FRONTLINE
COVERAGE OF CURRENT EVENTS™

IRAQI INSURGENTS
RESISTING AMERICA'S NATION-BUILDING IN IRAQ

Bill Scheppler

The Rosen Publishing Group, Inc., New York

For Nick

Published in 2005 by The Rosen Publishing Group, Inc.
29 East 21st Street, New York, NY 10010

Library of Congress Cataloging-in-Publication Data

Scheppler, Bill.
Iraqi insurgents: resisting America's nation-building in Iraq/Bill Scheppler.—1st ed.
    p. cm.—(Frontline coverage of current events)
Includes bibliographical references and index.
ISBN 1-4042-0277-3 (library binding)
1. Iraq War, 2003—Juvenile literature.
I. Title. II. Series.
DS79.76.S347 2004
956.7044'3—dc22

2004009283

Manufactured in the United States of America

On the cover: Foreground: On September 7, 2004, a Shiite insurgent holds a rocket-propelled grenade during a clash with U.S. troops in Baghdad, Iraq. Background: In May 2004, coalition forces secure a Baghdad power plant so that the Iraqi people's electricity will not be disrupted by acts of terrorism.

Contents

Introduction

Putting the Iraqi Insurgency in Perspective

By the end of October 2004, the United States military had suffered 1,122 casualties in its war with Iraq. One hundred and thirty-nine of those deaths occurred during major combat operations, from March 20 to May 1, 2003. The remaining 983 transpired over the course of occupation and peacekeeping operations, and most were the direct result of attacks by Iraqi insurgents.

When you hear the phrase "Iraqi insurgency" for the first time, it can come across as a simple concept, a single thing. When you begin to read about the insurgency in the media, it may seem incredibly complicated—too many things to grasp. But when you finally understand the insurgency, you realize it lies somewhere right in the middle. This book will help you understand the Iraqi insurgency.

The insurgency in Iraq is perplexing, but it is nothing new. A history of Iraq introduces you to the key players. Expand your view to include other countries in the Middle East, and you will notice similar conflicts happening again and again. Throw in U.S. interests

In this photo from March 31, 2004, an Iraqi boy holds a leaflet on which a skull and crossbones has been printed along with the phrase "Falluja, the cemetery of the Americans." Earlier that day, four American contractors working for a security company were ambushed and killed by insurgents, and their burned bodies were dragged through the streets of the city. Falluja was one of the most dangerous areas for coalition forces. Part of the area known as the Sunni Triangle, Falluja served as a seat of Sunni resistance and as a hideout for associates of the Jordanian-born terrorist Abu Musab al-Zarqawi.

in the Persian Gulf region, and you end up with the who, what, and why of the Iraqi insurgency.

Specific people, events, and circumstances will come and go and evolve. This book gives you the basic tools to help you catch up to the current state of affairs in Iraq and stay informed as the situation unfolds.

chapter 1
Appreciating Iraq: A Quick Glance

On March 22, 2003, Iraqis set fire to oil trenches in the capital city of Baghdad (*background*) in an attempt to use smoke to camouflage buildings from attacking coalition bombers. Founded in 764, Baghdad was an important cultural center in the Arab world for centuries.

The Tigris and Euphrates Rivers run nearly parallel courses. These two mighty waterways originate in the highlands of Armenia before coming together just below Al Qurnah to empty into the Persian Gulf to the south and east. Never flowing a distance greater than 150 miles (241 kilometers) apart, the rivers enrich the land that separates them, creating some of the most fertile terrain in the entire Middle East. (The ancient Greeks named the region Mesopotamia, which means "between the rivers.") For thousands of years, tribal groups flocked to this oasis, enticed by its rich natural resources. It was here in Mesopotamia, on its rivers' banks, that the world's first civilizations developed into existence.

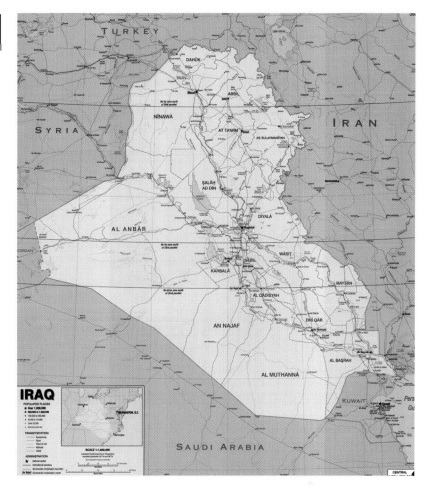

Iraq borders Turkey to the north, Iran to the east, Kuwait and the Persian Gulf to the southeast, Saudi Arabia to the south, and Jordan and Syria to the west. Its chief cities are Baghdad, which is near central Iraq and on the banks of the Tigris River; Basra in the southeast; Mosul in the north; and Kirkuk, which is in the northeast of the country.

Over the millennia as empires rose and fell, civilization continued to evolve in Mesopotamia, stimulated by such advances as cuneiform (the earliest known written language), the domestication of animals, and complex mathematic concepts including algebra. Indeed, as western Europe struggled through the Dark Ages, Baghdad from its perch on the shores of the Tigris emerged as the world's most intellectual city and richest trade center, connecting the Far East to the Mediterranean Sea.

Today, Mesopotamia makes up the heart of Iraq, and although the region lost its standing as a cultural center, its valuable resources continue to draw global attention to this enormously significant corner of our world.

Shia Vs. Sunni: Warring Islamic Sects

Following centuries of strength and influence, a weakened Baghdad fell to the invading Mongol army in 1258. Thousands of leading scholars were massacred in the devastating defeat, launching a long period of decline and instability in Iraq, which continued into the twenty-first century. Historians blame Baghdad's vulnerability at the time of the attack in part on internal conflict between its two major religious groups, the Shia and the Sunni.

Mesopotamia is sometimes called the Holy Land because it is largely recognized as the birthplace of modern religion. (In fact, many people believe that the fabled Garden of Eden was located where the Tigris and Euphrates meet.) During ancient times, citizens often worshiped their leaders as sacred idols, and on the Arabian Peninsula in the seventh century AD, one such leader—believed by some to be a prophet of God—founded a religion called Islam. The man's name was Muhammad, and his followers came to be known as Muslims. Shiism and Sunnism are two branches of the Islamic faith.

Upon Muhammad's death in the year 632 in Mecca, Muslims gathered to elect a new leader to guide them religiously and politically. The Islamic leader is referred to as "caliph," which literally means "successor to the prophet." Islam grew quickly, and the role of the caliph became quite powerful. So powerful, in fact, that when the time came to select the fourth caliph, two opposing groups clashed for control. One side fought to elect Ali ibn Abu Talib, a cousin and son-in-law of the prophet Muhammad. These people belong to the Shia or "party of Ali." (An individual member of the Shia is known as a Shiite.) The other group supported Muawiyah ibn Abu Sufyan, a relative of Uthman ibn Affan, the third caliph, and that division is called Sunni, which means "one who follows the way of Muhammad."

Although the Shia and Sunni have common beliefs based upon the teachings of Muhammad, ideological differences divide the two sects. This rift has only deepened with time and conflict, and much blood has been shed between the Shiites and Sunnis over their 1,500-year struggle for prominence in the Middle East.

The Kurds Campaign for Autonomy

As Iraq's most visible minority group, the Kurds, too, have a long history of struggle in this region—in the form of systemic oppression at the hands of the Arab majority. Kurdish tribes primarily inhabit an area that includes northern Iraq, southeast Turkey, and northwest Iran. Kurds have a unique language and culture stretching back more than 4,000 years, and at 25 million strong, they make up the world's largest ethnic group without its own independent state.

Britain defined Iraq's modern national boundaries following its defeat of the Ottoman Empire in the First World War (1914–1918). During the 400 years prior to World War I, Iraq and much of the region fell under the Ottoman Empire, which was controlled by Turkey. In the postwar Treaty of Sèvres (1920), a document drafted to divide the territory formerly held by the Ottoman Empire, Iraq and Turkey agreed to set aside a chunk of land straddling the two countries' shared border. This land was to become the Kurdish nation of Kurdistan.

However, before Kurdistan could be formally established, a new Turkish leader emerged and broke the treaty. Turkey reclaimed

the land it had promised to the Kurds, and Iraq followed suit, leaving the Kurds to exist as foreigners in both countries. In the decades since, the Kurds have staged numerous political revolts and been victims of bloody massacres as they continue to fight for self-government and the establishment of an independent state.

Rise of the Baath Party and Saddam Hussein

Without concern for the complexities of Middle Eastern cultures, the British drew national boundaries designed to inhibit pan-Arab unification and eliminate the region's ability to challenge British control. Ethnic tribes were divided, cities isolated from trade partners, and minorities elevated to positions of power. As a means to maintain order amid the chaos, Britain established a monarchy (government led by a sovereign leader, such as a king or queen) to rule the Iraqi people.

Anti-British sentiment coupled with existing hostility among Iraqis—Shiites versus Sunnis, and Kurds versus Arabs—made universal rule under a monarchy an unpopular form of government. The first military rebellion against the monarchy was staged in 1936. Others followed, and in 1958, the monarchy was permanently overthrown. Iraq endured an extremely unstable period for the next ten years until the Baath political party wrested control in 1968 and managed to retain power through early 2003.

Saddam Hussein, a key figure in the Baath Party, became president of Iraq on July 16, 1979. Less than a week into his presidency, Hussein identified members of his own party who he believed might challenge his authority. Those members were executed by firing squad, thus setting the tone of Hussein's reign: oppose him and die.

Hussein was a nationalist who wanted to see Iraq rise again in global importance. He spoke often of Baghdad's golden era and

While president of Iraq, Saddam Hussein erected murals, posters, and statues of himself on city streets to convince Iraqis that he was a caring leader. It is believed that during his rule, hundreds of thousands of Iraqis were killed or tortured.

Mesopotamia's role in the birth of civilization. Although he envisioned himself a modern, secular leader, Hussein and the majority of his loyal Baath Party members were Sunni Arabs confronted with age-old disputes between the Shiites and Kurds. In the end, Hussein ruled as an iron-fisted dictator.

chapter 2
The United States' Involvement with Iraq

An Iraqi oil field worker turns a valve at an oil field that was on fire near the northern city of Kirkuk in January 2004. American petroleum companies worked in Iraq as early as the late 1920s. The oil reserves in Iraq are the second largest after the reserves in Saudi Arabia.

The history of Middle Eastern cultures, politics, and religion is extensive and multifaceted. Indeed, the more you know, the more interesting it becomes, and the more it seems there is to learn. But why does this region of the globe—almost half a world away from the United States—play such a substantial role in U.S. foreign policy? The answer is deceivingly simple: oil.

Oil is currently the world's primary energy source. Global industry relies on oil, and international economies depend upon it, which makes oil the most important natural resource we have. Five of the top six oil-producing countries are located in the Middle East, and the region controls more than half of the planet's petroleum reserves. The British had this understanding in mind when carving up land to build nations in the early twentieth century, and it has been central to U.S. policy-making decisions since the close of World War II (1939–1945).

By 1955, the United States had established itself as a global leader, and American corporations controlled half of the oil pumped in the region. Most of the oil was shipped out to U.S. allies in Europe, making up 90 percent of their petroleum imports. Meanwhile, the U.S. government and military were already becoming active participants in Middle Eastern affairs, influencing political stability in the region as a means to regulate the flow of its valuable export.

Supporting Iraq's Invasion of Iran

Regional stability broke down in 1979 with the Iranian Revolution. This revolution resulted in the overthrow of Shah Mohammad Reza Pahlavi and the rise to power of Shiite spiritual and political leader Ayatollah Ruhollah Khomeini. ("Shah" is the former title of the monarch of Iran.) There were many similarities between the ruling styles of Shah Pahlavi and Saddam Hussein. Both were dictators who invested in modernizing their countries and adopted secular rule over Islamic law. In addition, both ruled nations in which Shiite Muslims held a two-thirds majority. It was clear to Hussein that the shah's fate could become his as well.

Donald H. Rumsfeld *(far left)*, a special envoy for U.S. president Ronald Reagan, and Iraqi president Saddam Hussein shake hands during a 1983 meeting in Baghdad in which the men discussed renewing U.S. diplomatic relations with Iraq.

The U.S. government shared Hussein's fear. U.S. strategy for maintaining influence in the Middle East depends upon the concept of nationalism (people identifying primarily as citizens of their country of residence and secondarily as members of a religion, ethnic tribe, etc.) as a means to keep large groups divided along national boundaries. Shiite Muslims typically identify as a single group; therefore, a subsequent revolution in Iraq could unify Shiites across country borders and begin to threaten Western control of the region.

In the 1980s, the United States, under the leadership of President Ronald Reagan, backed an Iraqi invasion of Iran. Over the course of the war, the United States provided more than $40 billion in weapons, technology, and intelligence support to the Iraqi

Iraqi soldiers battle Iranian troops along the border region of Iran and Iraq in July 1984. The Iran-Iraq War (from September 1980 to August 1988) lasted eight years and depleted both countries of valuable economic resources. It is estimated that the total number of war-related casualties was 1,200,000 people.

military. Although the war had no clear winner, the United States achieved its fundamental goal of avoiding a Shiite uprising in Iraq.

Shifting Allegiance Fuels Tension

The staggering cost of the war devastated both the Iraqi and Iranian economies. By the time of the cease-fire in 1988, Iraq was $75 billion in debt, and Saddam Hussein had only one option to pay off his creditors: sell oil at a high price. Hussein attempted to persuade OPEC (Organization of Petroleum Exporting Countries), the group that regulates oil commerce among its members, to require other oil-producing nations to reduce their pumping rates, thus increasing the price of oil by decreasing its supply in the marketplace. Kuwait, Iraq's tiny neighbor to the southeast, opposed the idea and helped persuade OPEC to reject Iraq's proposal.

Iraq owed a sizable war debt to Kuwait, which Hussein believed should be pardoned on the grounds that Kuwaitis, too, benefited from his invasion of Iran. Furthermore, he accused Kuwait of stealing Iraqi oil by slant-drilling under their

Iraqi soldiers waving white flags surrender to coalition troops in Kuwait in February 1991. The U.S.-led coalition, which included about thirty-four nations, launched a successful ground and aerial offensive to take back Kuwait after it was invaded by Iraq in August 1990.

shared border into Iraq's Rumaila oil field. (Slant-drilling is drilling at an angle; in this example it was the drilling at an angle from Kuwait's oil pumps to Iraq's oil wells.) Furious at Kuwait for contributing to Iraq's financial hardship and then hampering his ability to rebuild its economy, Hussein found himself in a desperate situation. Prior to the British-drawn boundaries of 1922, Kuwaiti land belonged to Iraq, so Hussein felt justified in taking it back.

In the first half of 1990, Saddam Hussein began mobilizing the Iraqi military and building up his forces on the border with Kuwait. At this time, Iraq and the United States still maintained open relations. On one hand, President George H. W. Bush's administration discouraged Hussein from using force against Kuwait, but on the other hand, it assured him the United States would not become involved in an Iraq-Kuwait border dispute. Hussein interpreted this as a green light, so when negotiations with Kuwait broke down completely on August 2, 1990, he ordered his troops across the border.

Almost immediately following the invasion—possibly inspired by the realization that with Kuwait under his rule, Hussein would control one-fifth of the region's oil reserves—President Bush changed his position. The United States demanded that Hussein remove his troops from Kuwait and collaborated with the United Nations Security Council to issue trade restrictions on Iraq. When Hussein refused to retreat, a U.S.-led coalition established a deadline: any Iraqi troops that were in Kuwait on January 15, 1991, would be removed by force. Hussein ignored coalition demands, and on January 16, the United States launched the Gulf War with a devastating air and missile assault on Iraq. Ground troops later surrounded the Iraqi army, removing it from Kuwait within a matter of days.

Hussein Emerges as an Enemy

From the moment he became president of Iraq, Saddam Hussein established himself as a ruthless and violent dictator. During his reign, he committed well-documented atrocities, including the authorization to use chemical weapons both on Iranians during the Iran-Iraq War (1980–1988) and on his own citizens to suppress Kurdish uprisings. Although coalition air strikes during the Gulf War destroyed a great deal of Iraq's military and civilian infrastructure, Hussein remained in power armed with U.S.-supplied weapons and weapon-building technology. Add to that a valid motive for revenge, and he emerged as a threat to the United States.

Following the war, the United Nations (UN) continued trade sanctions against Iraq to prevent Hussein from rebuilding his

This stretch of road leading from Mutlaa, Kuwait, to Basra, Iraq, became known as the Highway of Death during the Persian Gulf War in February 1991. U.S. forces bombed Iraqi troops that had sacked Kuwait City as they retreated along this road. Unfortunately, many civilians trying to escape the war also died on this highway.

military but modified the restrictions, allowing enough oil exports to support humanitarian aid for Iraqi citizens and construct vital infrastructure, such as hospitals and schools. Several other measures were put into place to eliminate Hussein's capacity for retaliation. A cease-fire agreement called for the dismantling of all Iraqi chemical weapons and other weapons of mass destruction (WMD) under the observation of UN weapons inspectors; no-fly zones, patrolled by coalition fighter pilots, were established above northern and southern Iraq to shield the Kurds and Shiites from further attack by Baathists; and in 1998, President Bill Clinton signed the Iraq Liberation Act, which states in part, "It should be the policy of the United States to support efforts to remove the regime headed by Saddam Hussein from power in Iraq and to promote the emergence of a democratic government to replace that regime."

chapter 3

The Overthrow of Saddam Hussein

Iraqis push the head of a statue of Saddam Hussein that was destroyed in Baghdad on April 18, 2003. The major phase of the war against Iraq began on March 21, 2003, and Baghdad fell to U.S. forces shortly there-after, on April 9.

U.S.-Iraq relations never improved after the Gulf War. Saddam Hussein refused to allow weapons inspectors full access to sus-pected weapons facilities. His regime routinely fired upon coalition jets patrolling the no-fly zones and continued to commit human-rights violations against Iraqi citizens. Conservative American leaders saw no hope for Middle East stability as long as Hussein remained in power, and they criticized the Clinton admin-istration for not taking full advantage of the Iraq Liberation Act to remove him. When George W. Bush became president of the United States in 2001, he filled the highest seats in his adminis-tration with the most influential of these critics, setting the stage for Iraqi regime change.

On September 14, 2001, U.S. president George W. Bush comforts a firefighter while standing on the World Trade Center rubble in New York City. On September 11, 2001, members of the terrorist organization Al Qaeda hijacked commercial airplanes and crashed them into the Twin Towers, causing the towers to collapse.

On July 31, 2001, six months into his presidency, George W. Bush submitted the following notice to Congress effectively extending Executive Order 12722 (which was drafted by his father, President George H. W. Bush, in August 1990) for the eleventh straight year: "The Government of Iraq continues to engage in activities inimical to stability in the Middle East and hostile to United States interests in the region. Such Iraqi actions pose a continuing, unusual, and extraordinary threat to the national security and foreign policy of the United States." President Bush had clearly begun to make a case for the removal of Hussein. The next steps would be convincing the American public and gaining approval from the U.S. Congress.

The United States Declares War on Iraq

Members of the terrorist organization Al Qaeda attacked American military personnel and civilians on September 11, 2001, by hijacking four commercial airplanes and crashing them into the Pentagon outside Washington, D.C., the Twin Towers of the World Trade Center in New York City, and a Pennsylvania field (en route either to the White House or the U.S. Capitol). The

This videotape obtained from CNN in August 2002 shows Al Qaeda leader Osama bin Laden with his bodyguards. Soon after the September 11 terrorist attacks on the United States, President Bush declared war on terrorism and sent U.S. forces to retaliate against Al Qaeda and the Taliban government in Afghanistan that supported Osama bin Laden's terrorist organization.

surprise assault was a wake-up call to the United States that, within its own borders, it is no longer immune to violence from its enemies in the Middle East. But it also revealed the critical degree to which stability was threatened in the Persian Gulf.

Al Qaeda is a Sunni Islamic group headed by Osama bin Laden, a wealthy Saudi Arabian. Bin Laden formed the organization in 1988 while fighting in Afghanistan against occupation by the Soviet Union. (Ironically, the United States was a financial supporter of Al Qaeda at the time because it shared an interest in the Soviet Union's defeat.) Afghanistan is 99 percent Muslim, and the resistance attracted hundreds of Muslim fighters from across the Middle East who opposed the invasion of any Islamic land by a non-Muslim force. Many of these fighters joined Al Qaeda. According to intelligence reports, Al Qaeda boasted more than 2,800 members representing at least ten Middle Eastern countries at the time of the September 11 attacks. Al Qaeda had successfully unified Muslim extremists across national boundaries and was beginning to strengthen its numbers by reaching out to Shiites. The timing was right for the United States to boost its nation-building efforts in Iraq.

The September 11 attacks both stalled and fueled the Bush administration's plan for Iraqi regime change as focus shifted from Saddam Hussein to Osama bin Laden. Shortly after the attack, President Bush declared "war on terror" and sent U.S. armed forces into Afghanistan to retaliate against Al Qaeda and Afghanistan's Al Qaeda–friendly Taliban regime. But once under way, the war on terror became a catalyst to rally support for military action in Iraq. In his first State of the Union address, on January 29, 2002, President Bush identified Iraq, Iran, and North Korea as components of a terror-sponsoring "axis of evil" and conveyed his intention to expand the military campaign into these areas if necessary.

Over the next several months, President Bush laid out his case against Saddam Hussein and on October 2, 2002, submitted House Joint Resolution 114 (HJ Res. 114): Armed Forces Against Iraq to Congress for approval. Citing intelligence reports (later determined to be unfounded), the president and his national security advisers alleged that Hussein had stockpiled WMD and maintained direct ties to Al Qaeda. President Bush concluded that Iraq "could provide these arms to terrorists." HJ Res. 114 received bipartisan support in both the U.S. House of Representatives and the U.S. Senate, which passed the resolution on October 11. By agreeing to the resolution, Congress took the final step toward combat operations, authorizing the use of U.S. armed forces in dealing with Iraq. And on March 19, 2003 (eastern standard time; March 20, Iraqi time), without the support of the United Nations or many of its key European allies, a U.S.-led

Top: President Bush (*top, middle*) meets with his war council in the Situation Room of the White House on March 21, 2003. Bottom: Smoke rises in Baghdad, as U.S. bombers begin their "shock and awe" attack on the Iraqi capital on March 21. The U.S. goal was to remove Saddam Hussein and his Baathist regime from power and replace them with a democratic government, eventually to be elected by all Iraqis.

coalition commenced air strikes on Baghdad.

Coalition Forces Take Baghdad

President Bush labeled the war Operation Iraqi Freedom because the end goal was to remove Saddam Hussein and his oppressive Baath Party from power and replace them with a democratic government representative of Iraqi citizens.

Clearly, the United States and its coalition members had the firepower and high-tech weaponry to defeat an Iraqi army weakened by two debilitating wars and more than a decade of economic sanctions. The challenge would be winning the hearts and minds of the Iraqi people while operating as an invading army and killing their fellow citizens. The invasion strategy, therefore, was three-fold: overthrow

English Version	Arabic Version

Front

Back

This handout, printed in English and in Arabic, was among the millions of leaflets dropped over southern Iraq on March 9, 2003. The U.S. military meant for the leaflet to discourage Iraqi troops from risking their lives against coalition forces. In other words, if Iraqi troops tried to attack the coalition troops, they would be destroyed.

the Baath Party with minimal casualties, dispense humanitarian aid immediately, and leave infrastructure intact to lessen the impact of combat on civilian life and the economy.

In an attempt to keep Iraqi deaths low, the coalition relied upon propaganda, precision, and speed. Media communications and millions of leaflets that were dropped on Iraqi troops from coalition aircraft promised a relentless "shock and awe" offensive and encouraged Iraqi soldiers to surrender rather than die on the battlefield. U.S.-led forces enlisted a precision "decapitation" strategy—primarily targeting military communication facilities and the highest-ranking Baath leaders—to defeat the regime from the top down. And with more than 70 percent of coalition bombs and missiles employing

An American soldier stands guard at a burning oil well in Iraq's Rumaila oil fields on March 23, 2003. Retreating Iraqi troops purposely set several oil wells ablaze in the Rumaila area, near the Kuwaiti border, to disrupt coalition forces. The U.S. Defense Department estimated that potential oil income to the Iraqi people would be more than $20 billion per year and would be vital for reshaping Iraq's economy.

satellite- and laser-guidance systems, collateral damage (unintended civilian casualties) was held at levels far below those seen in previous wars. Finally, speed was essential: the coalition lived up to its promise, thousands of Iraqi troops surrendered or scattered, and Baghdad fell three weeks into the campaign.

Operations to protect oil fields and to facilitate the delivery of humanitarian aid were equally important in gaining the loyalty of the Iraqi citizens. As soon as coalition forces neutralized Iraqi troops in the southeast, they set their sights on securing the port of Umm Qasr (Iraq's access to the Persian Gulf) to provide safe passage for coalition ships transporting humanitarian aid. Oil fields, pipelines, and facilities were seized and shielded from attack, thereby ensuring that petroleum exports could resume immediately after the war. These tactics were repeated as the campaign drove deeper into Iraq, and by the time coalition ground troops reached Baghdad, the road from Kuwait to the capital city had become a 350-mile (563-kilometer) lifeline of food, water, and aid for soldiers and citizens alike.

chapter 4
Occupation and Nation-Building

In Samarra, a U.S. soldier visits a school in 2003 after American troops refurbished the building. Coalition forces helped rebuild Iraq's infrastructure as well as its government.

On May 1, 2003, aboard the aircraft carrier USS *Abraham Lincoln*, President Bush declared victory over Saddam Hussein and his regime by announcing the end of major combat operations in Iraq. Although most Baath Party leaders had been captured or killed, Hussein's whereabouts remained unknown. (He would later be captured hiding on a small farm near his hometown of Tikrit.) Nevertheless, President Bush was confident Hussein would not return to Baghdad, and so began the U.S.-led coalition's occupation of Iraq.

Iraqi schoolgirls walk past a water supply project in Al Kut in 2003. The company in charge of the construction was an international nongovernmental organization (NGO). During the period of occupation and rebuilding, insurgents looked for ways to stop coalition attempts to transform Iraq into a stable, democratic society. They found NGO workers to be easy kidnapping targets.

Occupation is the state of affairs in which a country's day-to-day operations are managed by members of a foreign government within the occupied territory. Even though occupation begins when war ends, in many cases, it is more dangerous than active combat. Insurgent forces may continue to fight for the defeated cause, and occupiers—now focused on reconstruction—are easy targets.

In the aftermath of major combat operations, the coalition was tasked with persuading Iraqis to accept a new, democratic form of government. To achieve their objective, the occupiers would have to leave Iraqis better off than they were under Saddam's regime. Under intense pressure at home and abroad to quickly repair the war-torn country and transfer sovereignty back to the Iraqi people, the coalition vowed to do it in just thirteen months. But postwar Iraq possessed neither the tools to rebuild nor the government to run a newly liberated nation.

Coalition Provisional Authority

American L. Paul Bremer III arrived in Baghdad on May 12, 2003, as civilian head of the

The Central Bank of Iraq introduced the Iraqi 250 dinar banknote (*top*) in October 2003. The former banknote (*bottom*) depicted the smiling face of Saddam Hussein. The new banknotes, printed in six denominations, are based on designs that had been used historically in Iraq, before the Baath Party came to power. Such designs include an ancient Islamic compass and portraits of an ancient Babylonian ruler and a tenth-century mathematician.

Coalition Provisional Authority (CPA), responsible for reconstruction and humanitarian assistance during the occupation of Iraq. Armed with a budget of just under $20 billion and a vision for a unified Iraq that would serve as a successful example of stable democracy in the Middle East, Bremer functioned as the chief nation-building architect until the end of formal occupation. From repairing and expanding the national power grid to recruiting and training a new military, it was Bremer's job to ensure that Iraq be equipped to advance down the road to recovery.

Eager to show its commitment to the diverse needs of Iraqi citizens, the CPA established the Iraq Governing Council (IGC). The IGC was made up of respected Iraqi leaders—representing the Sunnis, Shiites, Kurds, and other groups—several of whom were forced to live in exile under the regime of Saddam Hussein. The council provided guidance to the CPA from the perspectives of differing religious and ethnic groups,

UNITED STATES AMBASSADOR TO IRAQ

On June 28, 2004, following the transfer of sovereignty to the interim government, U.S. ambassador John Negroponte became the top U.S. civilian official in Iraq. Prior to this position, Negroponte served as U.S. ambassador to the United Nations, where he tried in vain to gain support for the Iraq war. In his new role, Negroponte continues to court the UN as he attempts to secure international resources to assist in Iraq's nation-building. Although an experienced diplomat, Negroponte is a controversial choice to represent America in a country with a history of human rights violations. His critics accuse him of ignoring murder and torture by the Honduran military regime while he served as U.S. ambassador to Honduras from 1981 to 1985.

represented Iraq at UN meetings, and negotiated with the governments of neighboring countries. In theory, the IGC seemed like a great idea, but in practice, the notion backfired. Many Iraqis were not yet sold on U.S.-style democracy and viewed the coalition-appointed IGC as the beginning of a puppet government, one whose actions would be controlled by the United States. Two members of the IGC were assassinated by insurgents—an early indication that occupation, though short, would not be peaceful.

A member of the Iraq Governing Council signs the interim constitution in Baghdad on March 8, 2004. The signing of the document, which included provisions for Kurdish autonomy, by all twenty-five members of the council was the first step in handing over governmental authority to Iraqis.

Unfazed by the budding insurgency, Bremer followed his vision. He replaced Hussein's image on Iraqi currency with symbols from the country's history; encouraged the support of Iraqi institutions, such as the national symphony and soccer team; and established trade associations to persuade professionals from different backgrounds to build relationships based on common interests. Bremer executed a traditional U.S. strategy for the Middle East: encourage nationalism to ensure stability.

Interim Iraqi Government

Although the CPA worked tirelessly for more than a year on thousands of reconstruction projects, Iraqi nation-building officially began on June 28, 2004, with the transfer of control to the sovereign Interim Iraqi Government (IIG). The IIG is a temporary but complete national government composed of a prime minister, president, two deputy presidents, and twenty-six ministers overseeing government departments from health to justice to defense.

The IGC assembled the IIG as its crowning achievement before dispersing four weeks prior to the end of occupation. The IIG is made up of an impressive group of politicians, scholars, doctors, and business executives that mirrors the religious and ethnic diversity of the country. For example,

Interim prime minister Iyad Allawi (*left*), U.S. administrator L. Paul Bremer III (*center*), and interim president Ghazi Ajil al-Yawar (*right*) leave the June 28, 2004, ceremony in Baghdad marking the transfer of sovereignty from the Coalition Provisional Authority to the Interim Iraqi Government (IIG). The IIG will elect a transitional government in early 2005 that will remain in office until Iraqis elect a permanent government before the end of that year.

President Ghazi Ajil al-Yawar is a respected Sunni sheik, educated at Georgetown University in Washington, D.C.; Prime Minister Dr. Iyad Allawi is a secular Shiite and neurologist who studied medicine in London, England; one deputy president is a Kurd with a doctorate in engineering; and the other deputy president is a medical doctor and Shiite Muslim.

With the assistance of a UN team, the IIG is working toward the goal of electing a permanent Iraqi government by the end of 2005. This is an aggressive, multistep objective that begins with national elections in early 2005, in which Iraqis will select a Transitional National Assembly (TNA). The TNA, serving as Iraq's legislature, will draft an Iraqi constitution and choose a transitional Iraqi government to replace the IIG. This transitional government will remain in office only until the permanent Iraqi government election at the end of the year. Then, ties between a U.S.-appointed Iraqi leadership and a government that reflects the will of the Iraqi people will be severed.

chapter 5
Understanding the Insurgency

In the holy city of Najaf, an Iraqi Shiite militiaman shows the victory sign while taking a break (at the front line) near the shrine of Imam Ali. Followers of the rebel Shiite cleric Muqtada al-Sadr took over the shrine, one of the holiest pilgrimage sites in the world, while fighting U.S. troops in August 2004.

An insurgent is defined as a person who rises in revolt against civil authority or an established government. The revolt against U.S.-led civil authority in Iraq and the IIG has been constant since occupation began in May 2003. At first glance, the insurgency (sometimes referred to as mujahideen, the Arabic word for "strugglers") appears random and chaotic, but once you understand Iraqi history, U.S. relations in the Middle East, and the nation-building process, it begins to make sense—at least logically. As of this writing, the insurgency remains in a state of relative infancy. Key players will come and go during its evolution, but the main themes are constant and, in many ways, incredibly familiar.

In June 2003, former Iraqi soldiers protested and demanded pay when U.S. administrator Bremer dismissed the Iraqi military, which was mostly made up of Baathists loyal to Hussein. In October 2004, critics believed that Bremer's action negatively affected Iraq's ability to fill the ranks of its security forces and fueled the growing insurgency.

Removal of Saddam Hussein and the Baath Party from power took less time than coalition forces expected. Several Iraqi groups shared the United States' desire to overthrow Hussein's regime, and some even collaborated with U.S.-led troops to hasten his defeat. Iraq's Shiite majority believed it deserved a voice in political affairs; Muslim fundamentalists wanted Islamic law to replace secular rule; and Kurds longed for control over their tribal northern territory. But these same groups differed on the type of government that should replace Hussein's dictatorship, and the last thing they want is to have the United States determine their next political system. This is the root of the Iraqi insurgency. With no definitive administration yet in place, we are witnessing one of the rare times in history when the leadership of a country is just starting to take shape.

Sunni Baathists Continue the Fight

Sunni Muslims make up a minority of the Iraqi population, yet as the backbone of the Baath Party, they managed to lead the nation for thirty-five years. During their reign, Baathists were relentless in their violent repression of Shiites and Kurds. They have reason to fear a democratic government because the likely result of national elections is rule by the Shiite majority. Sunni Baathists have no intention of allowing Shiites the opportunity to turn the tables of oppression on them, and although Saddam Hussein is in prison, they have not conceded defeat.

Active soldiers and reservists combined, Iraqi armed forces totaled more than 1 million units prior to the 2003 invasion. The overwhelming majority of these troops were Sunni, and all were Baath Party members—a requirement by Hussein to ensure loyalty. Coalition forces killed or captured thousands of Iraqi troops during the three-week battle for Baghdad, but many more thousands simply scattered. The CPA dismantled what was left once occupation began, resulting in a flood of unemployed and disgruntled soldiers on the streets.

Some experts believe the scattering of troops was part of Hussein's original strategy. The United States expected the war for Iraq to be won or lost in Baghdad, but it would have been suicide for Iraqi troops to face the coalition head-on in defense of the city. It is possible the troops pulled out of Baghdad and into smaller cities to the west and north—the triangular-shaped area referred to today as

Iraqis loyal to radical Shiite cleric Muqtada al-Sadr carry pictures of the cleric during a rally in Najaf in August 2004. Al-Sadr has become known as a popular insurgent leader, and his Mahdi Army claims to have more than 10,000 fighters. The Interim Iraqi Government urged al-Sadr and his followers to support the elections in 2005.

the Sunni Triangle—with plans to regroup and resume the fight at a later time.

The motivation behind the Sunni insurgency is the preservation of Baathist authority in Iraq. In fact, rather than an insurgency, it could be seen as an extension of the original ground war conducted using guerrilla tactics. Sunni fighters continue to target coalition forces with roadside bombings, shoulder-launched rocket attacks, and other means, but they have the IIG and recently established Iraqi National Guard in their sights as well. The insurgents aim to inject enough disorder into the government so that Baathists can return to power before the democracy takes hold.

Shiite Extremists Battle for Islamic Rule

The Shiite majority stands to benefit most from a democratic government—if they want to. Iraq's highest-ranking Shiite leader, Grand Ayatollah Ali al-Sistani has been collaborating with the IIG because he values the influence free elections will bring to his people. But some Shiites disagree with the idea of democracy and refuse to cooperate. Rather than majority control over a secular government, fundamentalist Shiites demand total control under Shiite Islamic rule.

A Shiite uprising in Iraq was a possibility following the Iranian Revolution of 1979. In the wake of Saddam Hussein's fall, it has become a reality. The Iranian-backed Supreme Council for the Islamic Revolution in Iraq (SCIRI) encouraged the U.S.-led invasion of Iraq, and once Hussein was removed from power, they set their own plan in motion. Under the leadership of Ayatollah Sayed Mohammed Baqir al-Hakim, the SCIRI launched a Shiite insurgency in southern Iraq, attacking coalition forces with its Badr Brigade. Al-Hakim's movement was cut short when he was killed in an August 2003 car bomb attack linked to rival Shiite extremist Muqtada al-Sadr.

Al-Sadr has emerged as one of Iraq's most notorious and popular insurgent leaders—his Mahdi Army claims up to 10,000 fighters. Like the SCIRI, al-Sadr desires to create an Iranian-style government in Iraq. Specifically, he has taken steps toward converting the city of Najaf (a longtime religious center where the tomb of Ali ibn Abu Talib, who was a cousin and son-in-law of Muhammad, and the fourth caliph, is located) into a political center. Although al-Sadr's militia is responsible for many insurgent attacks, the IIG is wary of retaliating against him for fear of inciting even more violence. The government has instead invited al-Sadr to take part in the political process and seek diplomatic solutions to his demands. It is difficult to imagine al-Sadr's fundamentalist vision realized in a democracy, but time will tell for certain.

Outsiders Join the Mujahideen

The issue of how great a role outsiders play in the Iraqi insurgency is under debate. The Bush administration argues that most Iraqis favor the transfer to democracy and the major opposition comes from residents of other countries. Others say foreign fighters are few but manage to claim a disproportionate amount of publicity. What is clear is the fact that Muslims consistently cross borders to defend

Grand Ayatollah Ali al-Sistani's picture adorns a vehicle in the motorcade to the holy city of Najaf on August 26, 2004. Al-Sistani, the highest-ranking Shiite leader in Iraq, negotiated a deal between U.S. forces and al-Sadr's army to end more than three weeks of fighting.

Islamic countries against non-Muslim occupying forces.

Iranians have been linked to the Shiite uprising, and reports have surfaced that some Al Qaeda and Hezbollah (a Lebanese-based Shiite organization) members are taking part in the insurgency as well, but the outsider wreaking the most havoc in postwar Iraq appears to be Abu Musab al-Zarqawi, a Jordanian-born Sunni who, like Osama bin Laden, fought against the Soviet occupation in Afghanistan. Al-Zarqawi leads an Islamic extremist organization called Al-Tawhid Wal-Jihad or "Monotheism and Holy Struggle." His ambition in Iraq is to take advantage of the chaotic regime change to establish a purely religious Sunni Islamic state. To that end, Al-Zarqawi has three objectives: force the coalition out of Iraq, halt the budding democracy, and overpower the escalating Shiite insurgency.

Al-Zarqawi's followers have proven to be the most violent because they rely heavily on suicide bombings, they target civilian coalition workers as well as military personnel, and without national ties to Iraq, they are not opposed to killing Iraqis to achieve their goal. In early November 2004, U.S. and Iraqi forces launched a major assault on Falluja, an insurgent stronghold where military officials believed that al-Zarqawi and his followers were operating. The successful expulsion of Iraqi insurgents and foreign fighters from Falluja gave the IIG control of the city before the elections in early 2005. The Falluja attack also provided the IIG and American troops with intelligence information relating to the insurgent leaders there, their means of financial support, and the organization of some insurgent cells. In December 2004, the *New York Times* reported that Iraqi and American forces found documents and computers in Falluja that helped them capitalize on their efforts to hunt down the IIG's opponents, mostly former Baathists. Al-Zarqawi had left Falluja before the November attack, and military officials believe he is behind a new insurgent offensive in Mosul.

Kurds on the Brink of Rebellion

With the Gulf War cease-fire agreement in 1991, Kurds were granted political autonomy in the northern third of Iraq. Although they made concessions to the United States, this was the closest the Kurds had come to full independence. After playing a key military role in helping coalition troops secure northern Iraq during the 2003 invasion, many Kurds believed they had earned the right to an independent state. But with the transfer of sovereignty to the IIG and pending free elections, it appears this decision will be in the hands of the Shiite majority, which has no intention of parting with the oil-rich northern territory.

The Kurds have played a vocal yet cautious role in the emerging government, stating their demands and lobbying to have their autonomy drafted into the Iraqi constitution. If Kurds do not achieve liberation through legislation, they are prepared to fight for it—even if that means civil war against Shiites.

Conclusion

Regime change left Iraq without a national army, police force, or other defenses against armed militias. During occupation, U.S.-led troops assumed the duty of battling insurgents, while the CPA worked to establish a new Iraqi military—even going so far as to hire experienced soldiers from Hussein's former army. By the transfer of sovereignty, on June 28, 2004, Iraq had amassed more than 35,000 National Guard soldiers and slightly fewer than 85,000 police officers. But these troops were inadequately trained and unprepared to keep the peace, so the coalition and IIG agreed to keep 160,000 troops in Iraq to continue training the military and assist in efforts to disarm the insurgency.

In post-occupation Iraq, Iraqi troops answer to the Ministry of

Iraqi civilians cheer as Iraqi police march through the streets in Najaf in 2004. Rebuilding the Iraqi security forces and national guard in the fall of 2004 continued to be a challenge for the Interim Iraqi Government. Insurgents and suicide bombers persisted in attacking police headquarters and police recruitment centers throughout the fall of 2004.

Defense, not the coalition. In fact, U.S.-led forces now take their orders from the Iraqi military. This change of circumstances has had a significant positive impact on Iraqi soldiers and civilians. Iraqi soldiers patrolling the streets and confronting insurgents are beginning to feel a sense of national pride as they serve to protect their communities from violence. And civilians appreciate the difference between the

Iraqi National Guard and Hussein's army, which routinely interfered in personal affairs and systematically oppressed Shiites and Kurds. From certain angles, it appears Iraq has sown the seeds of democracy and taken great strides toward creating stability in the region and then—BOOM!—another car bomb explodes or another foreign worker is abducted, and you realize how much further the country has to go.

Glossary

Al Qaeda Arabic, meaning "the foundation," Al Qaeda is an independent military organization that is heavily influenced by its interpretation of the Islamic religion. Established by Osama bin Laden in 1988, it is widely regarded as a terrorist organization.

ayatollah From the Arabic "ayat Allah," which translates as "sign of God," ayatollah is used as an honorific title for leading Shiite clergymen who are qualified to interpret scriptures.

coalition An alliance, especially a temporary one of people, factions, parties, or nations.

independent state Also referred to as nation-state. A sovereign territory with internationally recognized borders, an organized economy and government, and external recognition by other countries and their governments.

Islam Arabic word meaning "submission (to God)" and described as a way of life and/or religion. Followers of Islam are known as Muslims and practice the religious teachings of the prophet Muhammad that are contained in the Koran.

Ottoman Empire Founded by Osman I in 1281. Originally a small state controlled by Ottoman Turks, the empire spread rapidly, becoming one of the world's most powerful political entities in the sixteenth and seventeenth centuries. The Ottoman Empire was brought to an end in World War I.

pan-Arab unification A movement for unification among the Arab people and nations of the Middle East who share a history, culture, and language. The group aim is to lessen Western influence and control in Arab states.

State of the Union address An annual event in which the president of the United States reports on the status of the country to a joint session of the U.S. Congress and outlines legislative proposals for the upcoming year.

Taliban Pashtun word meaning "religious student," the Taliban is an oppressive Islamist movement that ruled most of Afghanistan from 1996 to 2001, despite diplomatic recognition from only three countries, and that forged an alliance with Al Qaeda.

terrorism Commonly used term to refer to the calculated use of violence or the threat of violence against a civilian population for the purpose of producing fear usually for some political end.

United Nations (UN) An international organization founded in 1945. UN membership is open to all "peace-loving states" that accept the obligations of the UN Charter and are willing and able to fulfill these obligations.

war on terror Referring to several government initiatives and military actions primarily advanced by the United States to reduce the threat of global terrorism in the wake of Al Qaeda attacks on U.S. targets on September 11, 2001.

weapons of mass destruction (WMD) Weapons that are capable of a high order of destruction and of being used in such a manner as to destroy large numbers of people. They can be nuclear, chemical, biological, and radiological weapons.

For More Information

Embassy of the United States, Iraq
APO AE 09316
Baghdad, Iraq
Web site: http://iraq.usembassy.gov

United Nations
First Avenue at 46th Street
New York, NY 10017
(212) 963-4475
Web site: http://www.un.org

U.S. Agency for International
    Development
Ronald Reagan Building
Washington, DC 20523-1000
(202) 712-4810
Web site: http://www.usaid.
    gov/iraq

U.S. Department of State
2201 C Street NW
Washington, DC 20520

(202) 647-4000
Web site: http://www.state.gov/p/
    nea/ci/c3212.htm

The White House
1600 Pennsylvania Avenue NW
Washington, DC 20500
(202) 456-1111
Web site: http://www.whitehouse.
    gov/infocus/iraq

Web Sites

Due to the changing nature of Internet links, the Rosen Publishing Group, Inc., has developed an online list of Web sites related to the subject of this book. This site is updated regularly. Please use this link to access the list:

http://www.rosenlinks.com/fcce/irin

For Further Reading

Al-Windawi, Thura, and Robin Bray. *Thura's Diary: My Life in Wartime Iraq*. New York: Viking Press, 2004.

Fiscus, James W. *America's War in Afghanistan* (War and Conflict in the Middle East). New York: The Rosen Publishing Group, Inc., 2004.

Malhotra, Sonali, and Melvin Neo. *Welcome to Iraq* (Welcome to My Country). Milwaukee: Gareth Stevens Publishing, 2004.

Miller, Debra A. *The War Against Iraq* (Lucent Terrorism Library). Farmington Hills, MI: Lucent Books, 2004.

Murdico, Suzanne J. *The Gulf War* (War and Conflict in the Middle East). New York: Rosen Publishing Group, Inc., 2004.

Richie, Jason. *Iraq and the Fall of Saddam Hussein*. Minneapolis, MN: Oliver Press, 2003.

Shostak, Arthur B. *Making War/Making Peace (Defeating Terrorism/Developing Dreams: Beyond 9/11 and the Iraq War)*. Philadelphia: Chelsea House Publishers, 2003.

Bibliography

BBC News Profile. "Profile: Abu Musab al-Zarqawi." BBC.co.uk, July 1, 2004. Retrieved July 2004 (http://news.bbc.co.uk/2/hi/middle_east/3483089.stm).

BBC News Profile. "Who's Who in Iraq: Moqtada Sadr." BBC.co.uk, June 17, 2004. Retrieved June 2004 (http://news.bbc.co.uk/2/hi/middle_east/3131330.stm).

BBC News Special Report. "Iraq—A History of Conflict." BBC.co.uk, November 12, 1997. Retrieved June 2004 (http://news.bbc.co.uk/2/hi/special_report/iraq/29099.stm).

Cordesman, Anthony H. "The Iraq War: A Working Chronology." Center for Strategic and International Studies, April 14, 2003. Retrieved July 2004 (http://www.csis.org/features/iraq_chronology.pdf).

Filkins, Dexter. "Iraqi Leader Says He'll Respect Kurd Desire for Autonomy, at Least for Now." *New York Times*, June 10, 2004.

Filkins, Dexter. "New Government Is Formed in Iraq as Attacks Go On." *New York Times*, June 2, 2004.

Hirsh, Michael. "Racing the Clock in Iraq." *Newsweek*, February 9, 2004.

Hoge, Warren. "Security Council Backs Resolution on Iraq Turnover." *New York Times*, June 9, 2004.

Luft, Gal. "How Much Oil Does Iraq Have?" The Brookings Institution, May 12, 2003. Retrieved June 2004 (http://www.brookings.edu/views/op-ed/fellows/luft20030512.htm).

Risen, James, John F. Burns, and Neela Banerjee. "The Struggle for Iraq: Intelligence; Account of Broad Shiite Revolt Contradicts White House Stand." *New York Times*, April 8, 2004.

Sadler, Brent. "Reporter Gets Inside Look at Insurgency." CNN.com, July 8, 2003. Retrieved July 2004 (http://www.cnn.com/2004/WORLD/meast/07/06/iraq.insurgent.videos).

Thomas, Evan, and Rod Nordland. "How We Got Saddam." *Newsweek*, December 22, 2003.

White House Transcript. "President Bush Announces Major Combat Operations in Iraq Have Ended," May 1, 2003. Retrieved July 2004 (http://www.whitehouse.gov/news/releases/2003/05/iraq/20030501-15.html).

White House Transcript. "President Delivers State of the Union Address," January 29, 2002. Retrieved July 2004 (http://www.whitehouse.gov/news/releases/2002/01/20020129-11.html).

White House Transcript. "President Outlines Steps to Help Iraq Achieve Democracy and Freedom," May 24, 2004. Retrieved June 2004 (http://www.whitehouse.gov/news/releases/2004/05/20040524-10.html).

Wong, Edward. "Deputy Foreign Minister Is Fatally Shot in Baghdad." *New York Times*, June 13, 2004.

Index

A
Affan, Uthman ibn, 9
Afghanistan, 21, 22, 38
Al Qaeda, 20, 21, 22, 37
"axis of evil," 22

B
Baath Party, 11, 18, 23, 24, 26, 33, 34, 35
bin Laden, Osama, 21, 22, 38
Bremer, L. Paul III, 27, 28, 30
Britain, 9, 10, 13, 16
Bush, George H. W., 16, 17, 20
Bush, George W., 19, 20, 22, 23, 26, 37

C
Clinton, Bill, 18, 19
Coalition Provisional Authority (CPA), 28, 30, 34, 39

H
Hakim, Ayatollah Sayed Mohammed Baqir al-, 36
Hezbollah, 37
Hussein, Saddam
  fall from power, 20, 23, 26, 30, 33, 34, 36
  policies of, 11, 13, 14, 15, 16, 18, 23, 28, 33, 34, 39, 40
  rise to power, 11
  and U.S., 14–15, 16–17, 18, 19, 20, 22, 23, 26
  weapons inspections and, 19

I
Interim Iraqi Government (IIG), 30, 31, 32, 35, 36, 38, 39
Iranian Revolution, 13, 36
Iraq
  coalition occupation of, 26–27, 28, 30, 32, 39
  democracy and, 27, 28, 29, 34, 35, 36, 37, 38, 40
  history of, 6–7, 8–11, 13–15
  war with Iran, 13–15, 17
  war with Kuwait (Gulf War), 15–17, 19, 38, 39
Iraq Governing Council (IGC), 28, 29
Iraq Liberation Act, 18, 19
Iraqi National Guard, 35, 40

K
Khomeini, Ayatollah Ruhollah, 13
Kurds, 17, 18, 28, 31, 33, 34, 39, 40
  history of, 9–10, 11, 17
Kuwait, 15, 16, 17, 25

M
Mahdi Army, 36
Mesopotamia, 6–7, 8, 11
Muhammad, 8, 9, 36
mujahideen, 32

N
Negroponte, John, 29

O
oil, 12–13, 15, 16, 17, 18, 25
OPEC (Organization of Petroleum Exporting Countries), 15
Operation Iraqi Freedom, 23–25
Ottoman Empire, 9

P
Pahlavi, Shah Mohammad Reza, 13

R
Reagan, Ronald, 14

About the Author

Bill Scheppler is an award-winning freelance writer who has written on subjects ranging from the Internet to the Ironman, from Special Forces to civil rights. *Iraqi Insurgents: Resisting America's Nation-Building in Iraq* is Scheppler's sixth book written for the Rosen Publishing Group. Scheppler holds a B.A. degree in history, and currently resides in the San Francisco Bay Area with his wife, Emily.

Photo Credits

Cover © Ali Jasim/Reuters/Landov; cover (background) Courtesy of U.S. Army; pp. 4–5, 12 © Karim Sahib/AFP/Getty Images; p. 6 © Jérome Sessini/In Visu/Corbis; p. 7 Perry-Castañeda Library Map Collection; p. 10 © Setboun/Corbis; p. 11 © Thomas Hartwell/TimeLife Pictures/Getty Images; p. 14 © Getty Images; p. 15 © Jacques Pavlovsky/Corbis; p. 16 © Jacques Langevin/Corbis Sygma; p. 18 © Peter Turnley/Corbis; p. 19 © Oleg Nikishin/Getty Images; p. 20, 33, 35, 37, 40 © AP/Wide World Photos; p. 21, 23 (bottom) © CNN/Getty Images; p. 23 (top) © Eric Draper/White House/Getty Images; p. 24 ©U.S. Central Command/Getty Images; p. 25 © Reuters/Corbis; p. 26 © Chris Bouroncle/AFP/Getty Images; p. 27 © Paula Bronstein/Getty Images; p. 28 © Akram Saleh/Reuters/Corbis; p. 29 © Nikola Solic/AFP/Getty Images; p. 30 © Marco Di Lauro/Getty Images; p. 31 © U.S. Military/AFP/Getty Images; p. 32 © Saeed Khan/AFP/Getty Images.

Design: Geri Fletcher; Editor: Kathy Kuhtz Campbell; Photo Researcher: Amy Feinberg